MILITARY AIRCRAFT

AC-130-H/U GUNSHIP

BY JOHN HAMILTON

VISIT US AT
WWW.ABDOPUBLISHING.COM

Published by ABDO Publishing Company, PO Box 398166, Minneapolis, MN 55439.

Printed in the United States of America, North Mankato, Minnesota.
092012
012013

[♲] PRINTED ON RECYCLED PAPER

Editor: Sue Hamilton
Graphic Design: Sue Hamilton
Cover Design: John Hamilton
Cover Photo: U.S. Air Force
Interior Photos: All photos United States Air Force except: AP-pgs 18-19; Department of Defense-pgs 14-15 & 28-29; Lockheed Martin-pg 25 (insert).

ABDO Booklinks
Web sites about Military Aircraft are featured on our Book Links pages. These links are routinely monitored and updated to provide the most current information available. Web site: www.abdopublishing.com

Cataloging-in-Publication Data

Hamilton, John, 1959-
 AC-130H/U Gunship / John Hamilton.
   p. cm. -- (Xtreme military aircraft set 2)
Includes index.
ISBN 978-1-61783-686-2
1. Spectre (Gunship)--Juvenile literature. 2. Gunships (Military aircraft)-- United States--Juvenile literature. I. Title.
623.74--dc15
                    2012945705

TABLE OF CONTENTS

AC-130-H/U GUNSHIP ★ ★ ★

The United States Air Force AC-130H/U gunship is used to attack ground targets. It shoots powerful cannons and machine guns out of its left side. Because of its accuracy and advanced sensors, the AC-130 is one of the deadliest aircraft in the world.

An AC-130 gunship shoots flares in a training drill. Flares are used as countermeasures against heat-seeking missiles that may be fired at the aircraft.

MISSION: CLOSE AIR SUPPORT

The AC-130's main job is to help friendly ground forces. This mission is called "close air support," or "armed overwatch."

The AC-130 can fly in big circles over the battlefield for hours. When American infantry or allied forces need help, the AC-130 can strike with devastating power.

A U.S. Air Force AC-130U "Spooky" aircraft flies on a training mission with a special operations squadron.

MISSION: AIR INTERDICTION

The AC-130 is also used for "air interdiction" missions. This means it seeks out enemy ground targets, such as truck convoys. The AC-130 hunts the enemy with advanced sensors and radar. It uses its powerful side-firing weapons to stop ("interdict") enemy movement.

An AC-130H "Spectre"
flies a training mission
over New Mexico.

PYLON TURN

Aircraft normally use machine guns to briefly strafe enemy ground targets. The AC-130 attacks by using a "pylon" turn. The aircraft flies high overhead in a wide circle. The AC-130's weapons are always pointed at the same spot on the ground. When its weapons are fired, ground targets are hit with a continuous stream of bullets and shrapnel.

XTREME FACT

An important advantage of the pylon turn is that firing is very accurate. The enemy can be attacked even when close to friendly forces.

Ammunition fired from an AC-130U gunship explodes on a training field dotted with military vehicle targets.

VERSIONS

Today's most common versions of the AC-130 gunship are the AC-130H ("Spectre") and AC-130U ("Spooky"). The AC-130H is the oldest gunship, but it is very deadly. The AC-130U includes upgrades in radar and navigation systems. Both versions use the latest weapons technology. They can even track two targets at the same time.

An AC-130H "Spectre" gunship returns from a training mission.

An AC-130U "Spooky" gunship has upgrades in radar and navigation systems.

The aging AC-130H/U fleet eventually will be replaced by upgraded AC-130J and AC-130W gunships, which may include smart bombs and other guided missiles.

ORIGINS

The AC-130 was first flown in the late 1960s during the Vietnam War.

The C-130 Hercules (right) is a workhorse originally designed to transport cargo. Some were modified to become the AC-130 gunships.

The AC-130 replaced the Douglas AC-47 gunship. The AC-130 could fly longer missions than the AC-47. It also had better weapons and sensors for detecting the enemy.

An AC-47 "Dragon" gunship flies over South Vietnam in 1967.

XTREME FACT

AC-130 gunships destroyed more than 10,000 enemy trucks during the Vietnam War.

AC-130 GUNSHIP FAST FACTS

The AC-130-H/U gunship is a deadly aircraft used to support ground troops and destroy enemy vehicles.

AC-130 Gunship Specifications

Function:	**Close air support and air interdiction**
Service Branch:	**United States Air Force**
Manufacturer:	**Lockheed/Boeing**
Crew:	**13-14**
Length:	**97 feet, 9 inches (29.8 m)**
Height:	**38 feet, 6 inches (11.7 m)**
Wingspan:	**132 feet, 7 inches (40.4 m)**
Speed:	**300 miles per hour (483 kph)**
Range:	**1,300 nautical miles (1,496 miles, 2,408 km)**

WEAPONS

The AC-130H/U is armed with several powerful weapons. The M61 Vulcan is a six-barrel Gatling-style rotary cannon. The AC-130H is armed with two of these weapons. They can each fire up to 6,000 rounds of ammo per minute.

An AC-130 fires its weapons during a training mission.

XTREME FACT

The AC-130U uses a single 25mm GAU-12 Equalizer instead of twin Vulcan cannons. The Equalizer is a five-barrel Gatling-style rotary cannon.

The Bofors 40mm autocannon fires explosive shells. The larger 105mm M102 cannon can be used to destroy enemy vehicles, or even small buildings. Used together, these weapons rain deadly, concentrated firepower on enemy ground forces.

An image of an Iraqi plane being fired upon by an AC-130 gunship in 2003.

ELECTRONICS

One reason the AC-130 is so deadly is because of its sophisticated sensors. These long-range radar and imaging systems detect enemy ground forces even at night, or under forest cover. The aircraft uses a combination of television sensors, infrared imaging, and radar. It can even track two targets at once.

XTREME FACT

The AC-130 can operate during daylight hours, but most combat missions take place at night. The aircraft's sensors are a huge advantage when the battlefield is dark.

The AC-130 uses computers and motion sensors to navigate. The aircraft also relies on a Global Positioning System (GPS) to find precise locations.

CREW

The AC-130U has a crew of 13. Officers include the pilot, co-pilot, navigator, fire control officer, and electronic warfare officer. Enlisted airmen include the flight engineer, TV operator, infrared detection set operator, loadmaster, and four aerial gunners. The AC-130H version includes one extra aerial gunner.

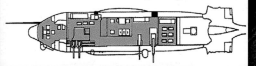

AC-130 Gunship Layout

AC-130 crew members work from their positions inside the gunship.

ENGINES

The AC-130 gunship gets lift from four powerful Allison T56-A-15 turboprop engines. Each engine has a four-bladed propeller. They are quieter than most three-bladed propeller engines. Each engine produces 4,910 horsepower (3,661 Kw).

Heat shields are mounted under the engines of the AC-130U. They spread out and hide engine heat. This makes it harder for antiaircraft missiles to strike the AC-130U.

An AC-130J under construction in Marietta, Georgia.

The new AC-130J model will use four turboprop engines that have a six-bladed propeller design.

RANGE

The AC-130 has a combat range of almost 1,500 miles (2,414 km). It can be refueled in mid-air by large tanker aircraft.

A KC-135 Stratotanker refuels an AC-130H Spectre gunship in midair.

Because of its long combat range, the AC-130 can fly in circles over the battlefield for many hours. When friendly ground troops need help, it takes only minutes for an AC-130 to respond with devastating covering fire.

COMBAT HISTORY

A close-up view of an AC-130 gunship flying over Honduras in 1987.

The AC-130 was first used in combat during the Vietnam War in the late 1960s. Since then, it has flown missions in Grenada, Panama, Bosnia, Somalia, Iraq (including Operation Desert Storm), and Afghanistan.
The United States relies more and more on special operations missions, where close air support is critical. The AC-130 continues to play an important role on the modern battlefield.

GLOSSARY

Allied Forces
Nations that are
allied, or joined, in a
fight against a
common enemy.

GPS
(Global Positioning System)
A system of orbiting satellites that transmits
information to GPS receivers on Earth. Using information
from the satellites, receivers can calculate location, speed, and
direction with great accuracy.

Infantry
Soldiers who move and fight mainly on foot.

Nautical Mile
A standard way to measure distance, especially when traveling
in an aircraft or ship. It is based on the circumference of the
Earth, the distance around the equator. This large circle is divided
into 360 degrees. Each degree is further divided into 60 units
called "minutes." A single minute of arc around the Earth is one
nautical mile.

OPERATION DESERT STORM

Also known as the Persian Gulf War (or simply the Gulf War). A war fought from 1990-1991 in Iraq and Kuwait between the forces of Iraq's President Saddam Hussein and a group of United Nations countries led by the United States.

SHRAPNEL

A deadly fragment of a bomb that flies through the air after the explosion.

SMART BOMB

Precision-guided weapons, also called "smart bombs," are bombs or missiles that can be steered in mid-air toward their targets. They are guided by lasers, radar, or satellite signals.

STRAFE

When low-flying aircraft fly toward and attack objects on the ground, usually with rapid-firing weapons.

TURBOPROP ENGINE

A turbine engine that uses hot gasses to drive a propeller. The engine also gets a small boost by recycling hot exhaust gasses.

VIETNAM WAR

A conflict between the countries of North Vietnam and South Vietnam from 1955–1975. Communist North Vietnam was supported by China and the Soviet Union. The United States entered the war on the side of South Vietnam.

INDEX